The Chronicler of Indifference

Bahloul

Poems translated from Arabic by:
Bahloul & Samantha Kostmayer-Sulaiman

Poems highlighted by § were written originally in English

Červená Barva Press
Somerville, Massachusetts

Červená Barva Press
P.O. Box 440357
W. Somerville, MA 02144

www.cervenabarvapress.com

Bookstore: www.thelostbookshelf.com

Cover Art: Kevork Mourad *(The Offering, 2015, ink on paper, 114 x 241 cm)*

Cover Design: Khalil Younes

Production: Allison O'Keefe

ISBN: 978-1-950063-85-7

Library of Congress Control Number: 2024934736

"...What surprises me is the liberty in which he writes his poems; creating new images, shoving new vocabularies in the ancient dictionary of poetry...Not only a buffoon bird, but also pain, disappointments, sadness, and futureless horizons. Thank you, for this fearlessness and sensitivity."

— Maram Al-Masri, acclaimed Syrian-French poet,
author of (A red cherry on a white-tiled floor)
[Karzaï ḥamrā' 'alá balāṭ abyad]

"The opening line of the Arab Surrealist manifesto of 1975 proclaimed: 'With disgust we shove aside the dregs of survival and the impoverished rational ideas which stuff the ash-can-heads of intellectuals.' While the author may or may not bear the direct or conscious influence of that movement begun in the 1930s, the tone and imagery of these eminently readable poems, ranging from the flippant to the wistful, with an updated pinch of post-modernist irony and self-referentiality thrown in, fashion poetry, and succeed in finding a universalism, out of the surrealist's rejection of the dual illusions of nationalism and rationalism."

— Alex Cigale, poet, editor, translator,
lecturer in Russian Literature at CUNY-Queens College

To those who remained. To those who left.
To Syria
and the endless shadows that dwell in between...

PREFACE

Existing in the USA nowadays is a visceral and painful exercise; admittedly the muscles of my psyche are out of shape. Countries attempt suicide, and there's no remedy to their cries. Poets, similarly, buy impotence by the pound in a bazar of useless metaphors and vintage images. Today, I find myself left with a partial image in my hand. A half-burned polaroid photograph, which looks like something from the past. Who are these familiar faces? And why handcuffed?

In the past decade, the denominator of my range of experiences in the USA has been to seek a news-proof shell and escape inside it. In that shell of parallel normative worlds and benign absurdities— I could still "tend to my own inner garden." Watering the plants with cynicism and reaping congenitally-defected coping-mechanisms. Poetry, in a sense, is the ultimate shell for an immigrant like me. And writing has been my defected coping-mechanism. I believe this creates, among many other things, a place for this poetry on the shelf of curious, or indifferent, readers.

In this book, I self-translated my poems— and later worked on each piece with Samantha. We would dive together into the images and metaphors. We would dismantle the polaroid and canvas off the wall of imagination and put them back together. She is my co-translator, and I owe her a lot of gratitude for this book. Self-translating my poems, however, was such an illuminating task. One that begs for self-referential understanding. A process extending beyond what the language can say into the unsayable. Into what has changed in me since I moved here. In this book, the influence of cultural hammering on my language and thinking is conspicuous. It's as if we were attempting not only to translate poetry in the linguistic literary sense, but also to reexamine and reproduce my emotional experience as my identity was going through a great transformation in diaspora. Some of the poems in this book were written originally in English—Samantha's editorial strokes were indispensable.

Finally, this book is not about Syria. The homeland only lingers in the background like an essential and necessary sky—but one that is relative and mutable. I invite you to read this book with open minds, and to play around with the concepts of home, identity, being, and belonging. Apply them to yourself or throw them away. Take them apart or put them together. I invite you to play freely like a child melding the Lego pieces of an illogical game-set we call—poetry.

Bahloul   *March 9, 2018*

CONTENTS

IV
Being Kaput

I
Reckon

Migration

I don't know what happened exactly—
what I've been told
is that I left Lattakia
in a mysterious way

some say I was smuggled
alongside migrants
illegal goods
local tobacco
and aged wine aboard an old Suzuki truck
to Turkey,   Greece,   then Hungary,
and miraculously   America,
           at last...

some say who left was someone else
someone who bears my name
           and a fake passport
who has my eye color
my curly hair
and an irregular poetic period.

whispering, others said,
I stayed behind somewhere discreet
           jumping roofs at night...
a thief looking for love
           in that schizophrenic town

cynics contrived other rumors
        that I died
chocking on my tears
        or dehydrated from excessive weeping
or overdosed on my pills and perished
a fortunate martyr
        liberated;
as they won't pray for my corpse

the insightful bunch
claim I never existed
for my absence to make such a noise...
and all that happened
        was merely a well-plotted dream
directed by Steven Spielberg

according to me
the protagonist of this anecdote
all I know is that I left the country
        somehow...
leaving behind
a tree
growing alone on marble-floor
        in a seventh-floor apartment
        with arrogant balconies
        that cleanse the drought of the Mediterranean
        with jasmine
and an endless thirst
in that land of mine

Seven pragmatic solutions for existence

Solution No. 1

Marry a European and get a passport
Only then, you can go back home
one day

change your name to Derek or Yamato
change your skin color
      Michael Jackson style
book an appointment at the plastic surgeon
      adjust your accent with the speech therapist...
      I'm sure, they'll grant you
a visa appointment at the
      US Embassy

Solution No.2

you should seriously consider it—
        waving at you
as if she's about to caress your cheeks
or maybe
        holding a drink
        that makes you buzz
                without a sip...
A human-size cardboard
of a mediocre model

make it yourself
        or buy it
or even steal it from a busy shop's vitrine
        it doesn't matter
make sure to arrange a seat for it
on that plastic rose-covered table
             where, alone, you spend your dinners

Solution No.3

you'll need plenty of it
in your empty nights
soft or rough
scented or not
white or black
it doesn't matter
any kind of tissue-paper
        will do

Solution No.4

a box of pins
        comes in a suitable size
        that guarantees a nice flow of pain

sitting in your shirt pocket
replacing your pack of cigarettes
        next to the doctor's script...
it becomes a habit
        to stick yourself with it
three   times   a day
before meals

Solution No. 5

place your ambitions neatly
in the southern corner
of memory—
an expensive   comfy purple couch, made of velvet
and let it sit, sluggishly under the light
collecting the dust of time
and the fur of weary felines.

Solution No.6

hire a cello player
with what dough you have left
and let her walk behind you
playing
> the musical background
> from your inflated life

Solution No.7

hit the dead with your stick
  poke the corpse
  perform CPR on it
  rent a room and watch her make love to a stranger
  arrange a place for her
    in your extended fields...
It will make a perfect scarecrow
  this fat corpse of existence.

A dark stain of decayed tomato skin

If you are looking for
great poems
          that harness admiration
for lustrous lines
          decorated with prizes
          and colorful gift paper...
then look elsewhere

if you are looking for traces
          of gunpowder
for portrayals of bullets
for the long stream of refugees
          digging   through   the chest of   the white continent
then look elsewhere
          and don't bother...
wars need no free advertising
dead languages care not about insignias

don't bother
you won't find a thing in here, except

          emptiness
          nil...
          no meaning
          no signifiers
          no symbols...
only dark reddened stains of decayed tomato skin
splashing the shirt
          of this innocent paper.

Caution

A sail into exile
or a flashback

a blind fold
the light peaks inside

this is how a traveler tells of the journey
a trembling road
a wall's memory of graffiti
rioting colors
and a machete cutting through the limbs of ink
Bedouins with face-tattoos
bargaining over gold-dust
in a market draped in seaweed
and the smell of peddlers' fish

this is how a traveler tells of the journey
    an image of a lake...
        exposed
    light reflecting on water
    hidden disappointments in homes,
    candles
        burning endlessly
        on empty dinner tables
        behind windows

this is how a traveler tells of the journey
    a migrant walking
        on vertical roads
    saluting the trees
    as they tell him
    of those who
    walked before
    and shed their leaves,
    the dry leaves
    stuck on their shoes
    stuck on his shoe from the contraband shop

here are twins...
    a migrant and a shoe
and the road whispers
in subtle signs
    "caution... deer"
a yellow sign at the side of the road
a sign at the margin of life
"caution... deer"
caution... postponed demise
a deer
    running against traffic
blind, facing torrents of light

this is how a traveler tells of the journey
       inflicting an excuse
       he eats his thorns
       he holds the Ney of his soul
       to play the tune again ... "da capo"
       only to entertain the stones of exile

tired
he enters his legal hole
he covers his ailments
       with a band aid
and arranges his dirty shoes on the ground
as tombstones of fellow travelers.

Cloud-Café

There,
          at the entrance of the chest
between a throat and a tongue
stands a   long line   of humans

workers in morose clothing
restless with weary faces
making plans
and strategizing hope
waiting for the end of war

frightened
        by
the price of bread and potatoes
and the cost of words

amused
        by
the concerns of global warming
and conspiracy theories
while Ebola butterflies
tickle the nose of their imagination
        until   they   laugh

their only consolation—
        a cigarette
and ashes
that drown entire cities

and when break-time is over
they draw crosses and middle fingers
        with the coal of time
on the walls of the lung
        then return to work

this is how the years of war pass
        one
                by one
falling
        like
                calendar pages

fueling his grandiose plans—
the lumberjack of lives
the bookkeeper of martyrs

he who answers the prayers of the
        dead
who with one hand
places medals on generals
while with the other
writes on clouds
        his poetry of lament

this is how the years of war pass—
        ordinary
nothing changes
        but the order of numbers

and the faith of those
      who chant in the streets

while up there
in cloud-café
somebody lifts his eyes
for a moment
leaning forward
to check on the loud noises
      from below
only to
bury his gray beard
again
      in his new iPhone.

A lemon-and-salt-flavored city

I have always admired
the sun's paradoxical logic
the way it colors rooftops
and scribbles with light
on the walls of consciousness

it has the reputation of magicians
in puppeteering astonishment
and luminous toys
between sunrise and anxiety

this is what belongs to me in this city
a treasure
hidden in an alley
next to the wheat-colored girl
under a chair
in a coffee shop

indeed
this is what belongs to me
tufts of my hair left in a comb
empty cologne bottles
a girl's greeting left hanging
     in the space
     between   two   buildings
a map of time
an afternoon siesta
before a snack of poetry and wanderings
     on   that   long   road

after the old toy-store
between *Hiyl Amerikan* neighborhood
     and the *West Port* gate
of the lemon-and-salt-flavored-city.

Sugar barracks

barracks selling sugar—
we buy our tooth decay
at their doors

we put the plastic of meaning together
one piece into the other
on an assembly-line

we shove slices of happiness
        in big cardboard boxes
and in automated moves
        we slap the "fragile" sticker
on the outside

inside street cars:
        exhausted humans
        slouching forward behind the wheels
        with their antiquated open mouths

by the way,
        have you ever wondered
        how urban skies
            unify humans
under one single   signifier
booming loudly
        "beeeeep beeeeep"

in these cosmopolitan cities
we become a baggy pair of underwear
with a loose elastic band
        sliding
down the silhouette
of aging lands
        exposing the delinquent
loins of
our supreme leader.

II
Play Dead

Co-existence[§]

They   live in peaceful coexistence
like some New-Yorkers
        and members of the squirrel species

They   live in different worlds of inner experiences—
he cooks her dinners
she pays the internet bill

they exchange passing looks every so often
and with curiosity
        they   watch
        life   passing   by
in this way
        exactly as it ought to be.

The hospice of the neutron

If my consciousness
creates the world
it, thus, creates you
and creates the love you
submerge

My consciousness;
the convert
the creator
the creature
the nursery of light, since the big-bang
the cemetery of romantic ideas about body
       and mind
and Descartes the dead...

My consciousness
the hospice of the neutron (N^0)
when I close my eyes
it reinvents you in microtubules
and vibrates
into a flamboyant bonny—after the world perishes
into a simpler land—after we all suffocate
into a faraway planet—glowing below the Andromeda
       and above Venus.

If my consciousness creates the world
it must measure the inclination of your nose saddle
it must document the frequency of your breath in (Hertz)
and observe the photons bouncing into your retina

You are my consciousness
the static
the recumbent
the dead
the living
the hospice of the neutron
its solipsism—in your image that remains but changes every time I see
that alters every time I remember
and fades every time I think

petri dishes[§]

blood-tainted agar
where the spoken word
grows
       more-or-less a thinking juice
       to genetically modify the poem
       the one that infuriates
           Jack Kerouac
so he chokes while biting his mountain-tops.

Marionette

Few days ago
around five to four
she perished in an isolated wooden cottage

days had passed
before the barking dogs
alerted her busy neighbors

down in the ground
she was put
hastily
on the hush-hush

no obituary, no nothing—
just like that
Madam Poetry had died

we grief her
like any other loss
we write her
only as if
we're learning a dead language
        as a hobby
        or to irritate our mothers
we await her rebirth
        in denial
like a cult of reincarnation enthusiasts

we sharpen our tools
as if we're getting ready for a clash
        of civilizations
we breed her metaphors in
        the stables of our minds
we laud her pros in our saloons
we recite the verses to our yawning friends
as we dangle Poetry's cadaver
from the empty puppet-theater — like a marionette
just so we can feel alive— for a precious moment.

Photocopy

Let me be clear
about these poems...

these poems are stolen,
a forged copy of the original—
a photocopy,
         you may say,
                  of the neural coda

the ineptness of language
prevents you   from tasting the *original*

like how paintings are photocopies
of the neuronal metaphors
         in the painter's mind

here, in this poem
I am a copy of this so-called "I"—
yet I'm not.

Stuff... stuff... stuff
poems   are   stuff—
pots and pans
filling storage cabinets
mass-production
         of emotion
rows beyond rows
of assembly lines
hurling to meet the production targets—

a delightful assortment pack;
poems for love
poems for self-loathing
poems to praise death
poems to praise this so-called life
made in China
or
assembled in Taiwan

cheap clones—
with un-matching plastic   edges
and an unpolished *emballage*

I admit that I try to make them bear more than they could do...
think of a red radio
        with an unbroken antenna
illusioned, I want it
        to swim
        to save my drowning children
        to purify the air
        from the sting of chemistry
I want it to do something
        anything
for the sake of despair—
yet all it does, is bringing me breaking news from afar

these exhausted poems are useless
tasteless—
a photocopy
a stillborn
You, who reads them—
my fellow *necrophiliac*...
you are savoring dead flesh
evident by the ink of words
lurking in the corner of your eyes.

Running for president

To live in a baseball arena
is an
endless   winter of poor connection

magnets on the fridge
a forest of postcards,
            trees, cities,
some visited, some not

too many clouds
and barely any rain

in this microcosm
you sign your speeches with baseball bats
and erase your mistakes with the fur of balls

in this microcosm
you imagine yourself an emperor
            to execute all your viziers
you imagine yourself a poet
            to erase the poems of others
and amused
            like any external observer
you become a soap bubble
cruising around this
deep   American
    bathtub

"deep enough, huh?"
deep indeed
like the melancholy which surrounds you

but only with a razor-blade in hand
you suddenly realize the thickness of dust   on your wrist

oh, how did I forget!
while you were writing all night
the most vulnerable creatures
            were running for president
            on TV
            and showing off
to their mass of supporters
the destructiveness   of   their   water-guns.

Deliberate slumber[§]

The comfy bubble around me
these bicycle rides on breezy August afternoons
piles of unopened mail
masterful issues of the New Yorker, never read
the tight and translucent workout clothes
and the loops of internet porn—ad infinitum...
all of it make me sleepy

the impotence of language
the pretentiousness of poetry
the limits of my compassion
and the dent marks on my empathy toolkit
...
all of it force me into a deliberate slumber

and I'll be remiss
if I don't throw in some words
      over this poem
like an orange-colored cone
      in the middle of the ocean
guiding the sailors— away
      from the meaning-zone...

      so here you go...
      "existential   angst".

III
Banal

A dead man writes a poem

I almost hear *Ares* screaming;
        "if god is sane,
he would've stopped this madness"
and this river which flows into no ocean
        is the heart that I borrow each day...

A stone
cannot stop a river
   a dead man won't light a stove
or reply to friends' e-mails

it's he who writes obituaries
and welcomes the mourners
        god, the absent
prepares arabic coffee
        in the last tent

Who knows how much a smile costs
        in the arms-market today?
Who knows the cost of a joyful song?

a curious child points to the sky and asks his father:
        "dad, look; are those helicopters throwing stars at us?"

a friend makes another fiery statement
before he disappears behind an ancient brick building:
"even in heaven
        someone   will   commit suicide."

Father's confessions

The night has lost its
wild berry taste
and the dawn has lost its
ancient ability to amaze

The soul takes a walk in the alley
where kids scratch its nylon stockings
while the stones bruise its feet

Nothing is like it used to be;
America is nothing like America
Lattakia is nothing like Lattakia

Seriously
I am planning
to put the world, and the rain forests,
the reindeers,
swine flu and ozone depletion,
beside pistols, rifles, and tanks,
cigarette butts, malnourished kids
and even hunger itself
on top of a pile of papers filled with confessions
before god and say:
       "sign here".

Death exercises

It was the spring of vivid details...
overdue appointments
lying on green grass
wearing a navy-blue shirt
buttoned with bullet holes
and redolent of gun powder

In the background;
a *basmala* in Yiddish
and some muffled
prayers

It was the spring of vivid details
the distinctive sting of wine
the vivacious chatter and silence of the wind
the dope of disappointments
of failures
of home
where the ball of flesh
        swells
running   down   a   hill
picking up screws and nails as it goes
home
where air is routinely arrested
and dreams are held
without arraignment

Don't ask him to look, he who had his eyes gouged
Don't hand him a trumpet, he with a punctured lung
Don't expect affection of him, he who carries a bullet in his heart

It was the spring of vivid details
of his mother's trembling voice
like a hiccup in the amygdala
crossing the Mediterranean
alongside boxes, images, and faces
with a child's voice singing:
"Oh Syria, oh Syria
Oh Syria, my Syria"

Here,

> he finds what he needs
> even
> in a tiny mom-and-pop
> coffee shop
> > while

there,

> people lose their bread and carnage
> in a country
> vast as god

Nevertheless,
home is
a daily
breathing exercise

Of love and war

Of love or war
women gossip at dawn?

about the sting of first love
or the number of martyrs
whisper those sitting in cafés?

of torn souls
or divine intervention
curse those who held a Kalashnikov?

imagine it,
it's really an interesting scene
       Mr. Chaos himself is our guest
       he sits on the sofa
and scratches the velvet cloth
       with his long dirty fingernails

The master of ease
       stretches his legs and orders coffee
"no sugar, no milk, please!"
       twirling his mustache
throwing his speculations around
       preaching an end

Of love or war
did Mr. Chaos speak that day?
you may ask...

Of love or war
screams the woman
while her newborn
exits her thighs
        a pundit,
                I answer...

Rumors

Stop all the rumors
about the ugliness of the world today—
about solitary confinement,
suppression of speech,
beheadings,
dead forests,
marching soldiers,
moral inflations,
and the inevitable rise of the robots...
stop all this noise, as

I must analyze the shape of the clouds
          quietly
and follow the changing colors of the sea

I must write about joy blossoming in the camps
about the scent of fresh heavens in the afternoon
and about a famous love story between two mosquitos
          meeting under a grass leaf, leave

me alone
let me fall
          freely
          off this cliff
of opportunities

as for this version of me— existence   is a
delicate
yet breathtaking
job
        like   drawing   on   two   narrow   wings   of   a   fly.

Déjà vu

What you won't see again
will forever reveal itself to you...
on the cold façade of tea cups
in the condensed water drops
in the hermetic crumbs
       under the pillows
in every text message
      that arouses your coma

what you won't see again
will forever reveal itself to you
in poetry dust
in black mug bottoms
in land flirting with oceans
in sailboats coquetting with fishnets

in a world like ours
in a possible universe
      that looks like ours

what you won't see again
  will haunt you
will choke your freedom
will arrest your imagination
—will shut you down
      by a remote control...

      The eye is open
      you can't help but see

A bullet-train full of celebrities

Life and what it passes on, remind me of you—
panoramic elevators
and Richard Dawkins' book about
      some selfish genes

weird vibrant colors
and that "hippie" scent illuminating the
air
roasted coffee beans
the texture of old books
the sound of a window squeaking on its track
      and
that moment when winter blows against the glass

life and what it passes on, remind me of you—
peoples' necks
      moles spreading on bountiful acres of flesh
      like a chair rocking alone
         on the porch of this universe

life and what it passes on, remind me of you—
Julia Robert's smile
Monica Bellucci's tan
and that wicked attractiveness of
      Scarlet Johansson

life and what it passes on, remind me of you—
dancing reflections on store fronts
hunger and crying babies
          the smell of french fries
and the taste of the blues after midnight...

so, it becomes a habit
that every time I sit in a bullet-train
going from B to A
I close my eyes
dismantle the wheels and windows
enter the memory space— and use your carefully uploaded portraits
to build a
          photo exhibit.

Hunter

Every time I hear jazz
        a spell is cast— I'm forced into the past
back to
        November Eleventh, 1958...

to find myself in a room
        leaning against a wall
at a specific moment
when a gramophone skids off the groove
and the music wriggles
        aloud

a random moment like a glitch
when the sounds stretch
        and the dancers slip,
with their long colorful skirts
and large suits
of white pocket tissues
like two mountain peaks
covered with snow

With the burning curiosity of time travelers
I try to decipher the title of a newspaper tucked in a corner—
the dancers get in the way
while the letters shiver on paper
        as they trickle down
        through the faucet of time
one   drop   at   a   time...

did anyone read beyond page six of that paper? I wonder
can any of the millennials recognize a single name in the obituaries page?
who was chased by police dogs that week?
how many black heads were crushed by the batons?

And above all
who forces me into this time machine?
what do they want?
who reincarnates my body
          with a loaded memory of past lives?
who is the lunatic that stands at the cliff of the abyss
          throwing a net
                    trying to catch a *moment* after it passes?

IV
Being Kaput

Delirium

White stripes cover the streets...
           what magic...
especially when they pass like rabbits...

sixth grade
a book of science
           with flowers that don't wither

bedtime and a careless plunge
           into   pages
over a blue sea of maps

fully dressed
           mounting
           a broomstick;

childhood is like writing a question today
that you forget tomorrow
or like a small notebook full of unsolved riddles

like engraving on your heart
for no good reason
"no photography allowed"

it's more like god returning from the telltale
after   smuggling   some   hope
           to his people

looking through a hole
        squeezing his nose
mocking this universe

"do I have to marry a Jew to become Jewish?"
said the lady sitting in front of me
in Bus No. 65 heading towards Downtown Houston
and expecting no answer
she   turned her head
and   morphed   into   a
cloud.

In the empty goal

in consciousness, I start
        under the sheets, I end

lonely like a prime number
groggy like an antenna through a storm

I mean
        like a bird who buffoons
        who paints his face with colors
and uses his eyes
to lick the spilled blood off the table

have you noticed lately
how the air tastes like raw peaches
and how
        the look on that bird's face
resembles a big white hole?

"where is this poem going?"
"where did I lose my car keys?"
"what color is your underwear today?"
my imperative questions
start in the consciousness
and end up as vomitus
            in the belly of the sink

plus, there is no point in tricking Night
isn't it god wearing
black?

the bird buffoons
the bird hacks
the bird dies of diabetes...

alas,
when you leave this world—
you asshole,
I will place the planet
on a white chalk dot
and kick it firmly,
        in the empty goal.

Where do I find an opener for canned hope?

You open your windows in the morning
the light tears up your retina
and burns   all   the   way
        to the brain

boredom sneaks up on you
        like white ants under the pillow
to devour your awakening

breakfast today— scrambled eggs
and a fiasco!

This is a balcony
a fifth dimension
        with open possibilities
        like a lottery ticket folded
        in your wallet
the sea is fake-reassurance
and the far away waves
are phlegm of a pagan god sick with the flu

You rub your eyes as hard as you can...
where can I find an opener for canned hope?

She knows
that you don't know
how hard is it for you to be
as
          no flower grows
               on hamburger

Faceless automobiles   pass   the   street
across from the coffeehouse...
you're almost out of gas
and the forest
          has promised its last children
to *Al-imam Al-Moughrabi*
and there is nothing left in your hand
          for which you can bargain
except a tiny little cartilage

how can you then stop rush-hour traffic
          with your finger?

The beauty of *ends*
is
          their   tardiness
the triviality of *beginnings*
is
          that they show up before everybody
and they both know
that holding hands
on the corniche
is against the laws of physics

At public cocktail parties
the *end* controls you
like a brunette
on a bed of lust

my dear,
when you leave the bedroom
be courteous to others
and
          tie   your   end
to the leg of the chair.

I will arrive alive this time

Wait for me
on the sloping road
leading to the corniche
and when I arrive
      don't vent

wait for me
I'm coming despite your storm

and even if
you try to hide your resentment
you will keep on waiting...
arrival is a curse
      on a traveler in a silk-winged carriage

There
on the same street
next to the old church
      under
the yellow glow of the lampposts
where I celebrated my birthdays
there's an insomniac ghost
who places his followers
      at the corners
      to stare at people
while smoking and drinking beers
in cans wrapped in black bags

they know everybody
even if they pretend not to...

Your local eyes
are vases of murky sea water
and their blinking is the divergence
of the sea at the feet of our city

Wait for me
even if I am forced to pass
I will come properly
passing   through   the   hole   of   memory
and I will arrive alive
            this time.

Upcycled[§]

Totems on the table
      and kids' writings on the wall.
Guidelines are being made.

A hammock made of imaginary fibers
      under clouds as macrocosms.
Your loneliness is a tenant.

Voices mimicking the wind—
is it the relative silence of vending-machines selling me candy bars,
or the roar of the alphabet protesting the totalitarianism of logic?

Where did you lose the muse, you cheap bastard?
When did you start selling recycled punch-lines?
Look in the drawer, or next to the coffee mugs,
      look on your hairy chest,
         there,
            over the bullet scar.

Hemiplegia

For him,
the doors open voluntarily
and the bus always
arrives on time

for me,
existential dread
and flocks of butterflies
I breed in my stomach

for him,
dry rain
and the blossom
of all women

for me,
hurricanes
floods
and piles of un-used condoms

a spark in his eyes
keeps the universe in its shell...
the expanding universe
on a bed of eternity

the stretching universe
that raises its head,
         contemptuously
every time a far planet breaks wind

my foe, sits like a fox
and thinks about the mechanism
         in which trains could fly
and the tricks needed to teach dogs how to speak
while I think about trains as metaphors of escape
and how dogs are the modern-day concubines

he is the original coin
I am the left-over sandwich in the office fridge
he is Uranus
and I'm not even Pluto

so you won't be surprised to hear this...
while the sexy Italian was whispering in his ear:
"you are my little Stellina"
I was in an Irish pub, drinking a beer
spreading my forgery tool-kit
and carefully affixing my name
to the cover of some forgotten book.

Kaput

The poetry-machine is kaput.
Time— the white papermill
ripples in a mute printer.

In moments like these
the sky may suddenly
become *prima facie*!
and thoughts become children
      playing peek-a-poo
      in the flank of the city
throwing   stones in
      her kidneys

I digress...
    but when I expire
as an audience—
please
    open the door
and run out
I beg you—
    don't sit
at the edge of your chair
and drain   me   like   this

as the evening has started to yawn and scratch its head,
I suggest I end this prayer
with an inappropriate gesture

and as you have started to get on my nerves with this poem
I'll declare coldly:
        "no one lives in the coffee-table, so don't escalate your knocking on it"

there is a parallel universe
       where I live using a different character,
a fake identity of
       an obsessive-compulsive mortician,
an embalmer of prose...

where
I have a luxurious room
with ornamented walls
a large fireplace
and a rocking chair

poetry is my room that I barely enter

alright poetry
you now have all the good reasons to
kill me
but please do so   after   you wash   your filthy hands.

Severed[§]

How can I explain to my mother
    that solitude is unique too?

how can I explain to my brother
    this indifference?

how can I create any meaning
    while my words are being pureed for the next man's dinner?

how can I fathom anything
    in these scrabble-filled chronicles?

Well,
    here's a caricature of my meaningful life:
    trembling and thrilled, I keep eye contact with whoever's
        running
            towards
    my deliberately escaping–
            spaceship.

Dear reader,

If you have managed to read through these poems, I thank you and admire your tenacity. I don't like these poems, but I grew to love them enough that I want to share them with you. And I imagine you might have some questions for me after reading. You may want to know the history of the poems, the order in which I wrote them, and their origins. You may be curious about what inspired each one and how did it develop. But I don't remember much of those years to construct any rich historical account. You can try to quiz me all night about each poem and I will oblige. I am a very openminded person and could be easily persuaded with a good argument. You can possibly convince me that one poem or another was said many times before, stolen, or even written by artificial intelligence. Anything is possible! When thinking about these poems, I simply do not recall anything to be certain. Nor can I ever be. Memory is a tricky thing.

To be clearer, this book was forgotten by me before I suddenly decided to publish it. Like anything that is no longer useful in the world, this book was hidden in a sealed box, up the memory attic, with the door shut tight. I tried to forget about it like a child who is closing his eyes forcefully believing the world will no longer exist when he stops looking. I was making promises to my publisher to finalize the manuscript, and consistently breaking them. Anyway, what made me decide to publish it today, is not well-defined, like many causes of trivial or great events. But so it happened that I pulled out these poems from the attic, cleaned the dust of time over them, and here I am trying to write you something about them. What do I really know about what was forgotten?

First, let me be clear about one thing. The situation of my memory is not that bad. Say, if you ask me: "When did you write this or that poem," I would not know precisely, but I can give you some generalities and make educated guesses. And that's all anyone can do. Especially that it took me a third of my life on this planet to complete these poems. Waves and waves of writing and rewriting. Years of revisions and cycles of self-translating.

What I also know for sure, is that I did not steal poems, and artificial intelligence did not participate in the writing this book. I think I am convinced of that. Haha ☺ What I can also say is that I started writing some of these poems when I was still in Syria, right before I immigrated to the US as a physician in training to become a psychiatrist in 2008. That period saw the start of my relationship with Alma, my life partner who had a great influence in the making of my first published poetry book in Arabic "The Opener of Canned Hope" (2008). A book which was to me like a debt I had to pay to homeland at a moment of voluntary departure. A pulse of poems gushed over a short period of time. Hardly few weeks. I was preparing physically and mentally for immigration— but I made time to write. When it was out, I signed the book in a small ceremony of friends and family in "prose poem café" and literally took the flight out.

Many of the poems from "The Opener" appear here in English, but you have also read poems from my second book in Arabic, "Birds Smoking Marijuana" (2017)— a heterogenous collection written after my immigration. Also, many English poems you have read here were unpublished anywhere else before. Needless to say, the writing of this book took place over the years between two main locations. Syria and the United States. Some poems were written back home in Latakia, some in Houston. Some in New Haven, others in Dallas. It is an amalgam of time condensed into one poetic moment after another, with an irregular pulse. Like that of a dying man. Like all of us.

The birth of this version of *The Chronicler of Indifference*— came as a collaboration with Samantha Kostmayer-Sulaiman, my co-translator. In 2013, I was invited to recite some of my self-translated poems with a group of Syrian poets in New York City. At the time I was a fellow psychiatrist, addictionologist in training, exhausted yet exhilarated by the clinical work I was doing on the forefront of the opioid epidemic in the United States, and the relief work I was doing with Syrian refugees across the oceans. I was eager for an outlet to my growing nihilistic tendencies after bearing witness to such suffering in the world— bordering on despair. I was excited to be included and given the space to read my poems. I was ushered into this small group of Syrian poets in diaspora and had the privilege to start working with Samantha on the translations in this long process.

The last thing I can say for certain about this book is the very last thing I wrote in it— which was the preface dated March 2018, when I first sent the book to my dear editor Gloria. The preface captures my mental state at a moment in time, living in Trump-America, and getting ready to relinquish poetry for good. At the time, I thought I was ready to pay the debt of a long difficult decade, but little did I know that the book will not see daylight until years after.

Since March 2018, a lot had happened—I drifted to music and buried this book. A Global pandemic hits. I become a father. And an ecological disaster arrives at our doors, etc. etc. Just life, merely passing by as these poems were completely out of my conscious mind— forgotten. Until a week ago, when I picked them up again to read and experience visceral reactions ranging from joyful to nostalgic smile, and from cringe to squeak. I want to admit to you, my dear reader, that today while I was preparing this final version of the book for publishing, I had understandable urges to take some poems out, and to try and rewrite others. Many poems say things I no longer wish to say. But I tried to resist the urge, and somewhat succeeded. I read the poems again and again and revisited the tender emotional points of each one. Gradually, with minor editorial strokes, the ugly and repulsive became more tolerable. And the book familiar and homier. The last touch I put on this book was rearranging the poems in four sections, and then sitting to write you this letter. What I want to say here, is that while I may dislike these poems, reengaging with my past made me able to accept it, and love these poems as testimonies of a former life.

Many feel the same about their older images. Our self-image is always changing, and so is our appreciation of certain things. I appreciate today how cynical and angry I was during those years, and maybe that's one reason I don't like these poems. To read old poems of yours, is to appreciate the effect of temporality through change.

So which poem I wrote first, or last? Does it really matter? It does not. What matters is that this is an attempt at using poetry to say something in this world. No matter how useless it may seem, a lot of good-use can come out of sharing... And if you are still curious about what prompted me after all these years to publish this forgotten book, I can now share with you that it has to do with an impending trip back home— an insisting urge to yet pay another debt.

So, wish me luck in my journey...
Yours truly,

Bahloul   September 10, 2023

Bahloul (A.k.a Hussam Jefee-Bahloul) is a poet, musician and psychiatrist. He was born in Syria in 1983 and currently practices and teaches at the University of Massachusetts Medical School. He writes poems and essays both in Arabic and English. He has two books of poetry published in Arabic, and has published essays in both languages. Bahloul is also a musician and songwriter. His project "Ta'sheeq" aimed at dovetailing the elements of poetry, music and visual arts together. The project toured many cities and performed around the US between 2015-2018. His current musical project Souq El-Jum3a (Friday Market) is a musical collective that aims at making original Arabic music keeping up the spirit of classical songs.

Samantha Kostmayer is a writer, editor, educator, and translator from New York City. She graduated from Columbia University, CUNY, and the American University in Cairo with degrees in history, forced migration, and law; Samantha is currently completing her Ph.D in philosophy. She is writing a volume of short stories and her translations have appeared in various literary journals and anthologies. Her poetry has appeared in English, Swedish, and Croatian.

www.ingramcontent.com/pod-product-compliance
Lightning Source LLC
Chambersburg PA
CBHW032106080426
42733CB00006B/444